FLOWER MANDALAS
COLORING BOOK

Stunning Designs on a
Dramatic Black Background

MARTY NOBLE

DOVER PUBLICATIONS, INC.
MINEOLA, NEW YORK

D1122595

Mandalas are symmetrical designs that represent the universe, and are used as a tool in meditation by many cultures. These carefully constructed patterns bring enlightenment to the viewer. Originally found in the ancient teachings of the Buddhist and Hindu religions, the timeless mandala is recognized throughout the world for its spiritual content as well as its enchanting beauty. The thirty-one mandalas included here all feature the splendor and wonder of flowers. The pages in this book are unbacked so that you may use any media for coloring, and are perforated for easy removal.

Bibliographical Note
Flower Mandalas Coloring Book: Stunning Designs on a Dramatic Black Background, first published by Dover Publications, Inc., in 2016, is a republication in one volume of all sixteen plates from *Floral Mandalas Stained Glass Coloring Book* (2011), eight plates from *3-D Mystic Mandalas Coloring Book* (2011), and seven new plates specially created for this volume by Marty Noble.

International Standard Book Number
ISBN-13: 978-0-486-80469-9
ISBN-10: 0-486-80469-0

Manufactured in the United States by RR Donnelley
80469002   2016
www.doverpublications.com

6. The book, which is about personality types, is really interesting.
7. (no commas)
8. My boyfriend, who hates parties, actually agreed to go to one with me.

EXERCISES 9–12

Answers will vary.

UNIT 14 (pages 221–235)

AFTER YOU READ

A. 1. translation
 2. generation
 3. poverty
 4. connection
 5. issue
 6. immigrant
B. 1. Hoffman
 2. Fong-Torres
 3. Hoffman
 4. Hoffman
 5. Hoffman
 6. Hoffman and Fong-Torres
 7. Fong-Torres
 8. Hoffman and Fong Torres

EXERCISE 1

The kitchen is usually steamy with large pots of soup cooking on the wood stove for hours, or laundry being boiled in vats for greater whiteness; behind the kitchen, there's a tiny balcony, barely big enough to hold two people, on which we sometimes go out to exchange neighborly gossip with people peeling vegetables, beating carpets, or just standing around on adjoining balconies. Looking down, you see a paved courtyard, in which I spend many hours bouncing a ball against the wall with other kids, and a bit of garden, where I go to smell the few violets that come up each spring and climb the apple tree, and where my sister gathers the snails that live under the boysenberry bushes, to bring them proudly into the house by the bucketful. . . .

Across the hall from us are the Twardowskis, who come to our apartment regularly. . . . I particularly

like the Twardowskis' daughter, Basia, who is several years older than I and who has the prettiest long braids, which she sometimes coils around her head. . . .

• • • • •

B.

Pani Konek teaches at the Cracow Music School, which I've been attending for two years—ever since it has been decided that I should be trained as a professional pianist. I've always liked going to school. At the beginning of the year, I like buying smooth navy blue fabric from which our dressmaker will make my school uniform—an anonymous
that
overdress we are required to wear over our regular
^
clothes in order to erase economic and class distinctions; I like the feel of the crisp, untouched notebook . . . and dipping my pen into the deep inkwell in my desk, and learning how to make oblique letters. It's fun to make up stories about
that OR *who* OR *whom*
the eccentric characters I know, or about the
^
that OR *which*
shapes icicles make on the winter windows, and
^
try to outwit the teacher when I don't know something, and to give dramatic recitations of
that OR *which*
poems we've memorized. . . .
^

EXERCISE 2

 2. who(m) . . . stayed
 3. when . . . was
 4. which . . . had
 5. that (OR which) . . . wanted
 6. where (OR in which) . . . were
 7. who(m) . . . take care of
 8. that (OR which) . . . put
 9. that (OR which) . . . have
 10. that (OR which) . . . find

EXERCISE 3

 2. where (OR in which) I drank coffee every day.
 3. whose sister I knew from school.
 4. that (OR which) many students attended.
 5. that (OR which) I hoped would continue to grow.
 6. when I had to leave Cracow.

EXERCISE 4

 2. [comma] when their marriage was arranged by relatives.
 3. [comma] where (OR in which) there was a large Chinese community.